CONDITIONAL CLAUSES

NOTE LEGAL

Due to the Internet's tendency to change quickly, the Publisher has made an effort to be as accurate and thorough as possible when creating this report, but he does not at any time guarantee or suggest that the information included within is correct.

Although every effort has been taken to verify the material in this book, the Publisher makes no guarantees as to the accuracy or completeness of the information and disclaims all liability for any mistakes, omissions, or incorrect interpretations of the content. Any seeming slights towards individual people, groups, or organizations are inadvertent.

Like everything else in life, there are no promises of income made in books with practical advice. Readers are advised to respond based on their own judgment on their own circumstances and take appropriate action.

This book is not meant to be a source for accounting, financial, legal, or business advice. We strongly suggest all readers to consult with qualified experts in the disciplines of law, business, accounting, and finance.

This book is recommended for printing for ease of reading.

Foreword

Through the use of inner resources you might not be aware of, this course aims to assist you in achieving financial success. You will discover through the 10 chapters that make up the course that you may stay focused and influence others such that success comes more easily and with less effort by shifting your vibrations and emotional frequencies from the bad to the positive. Learn all you require right here.

Financial Prosperity Technique

Find Your Wealth Frequency and What Suits You Best

Chapter 1:

Introduction

Do you think that wealth frequencies or vibrations even exist? These days, it seems that having enough finances, motivation, and talents are no longer enough to achieve prosperity or your overall goals. It's crucial to have the proper brain waves; in fact, it could be the most crucial of all.

How often does wealth occur?

According to studies, meditation causes the brainwaves to slow down to a frequency that is optimum for concentration and relaxation. Low alpha is the name for this. To attain theta frequency, which is optimal for manifesting or lucid dreaming, you can also reduce your brain waves. However, experts advise increasing your brain waves to tune in to the wealth frequency.

Emotional Wavelengths

David calculated the frequencies of human emotions from 20 to 1,000 in his book Power vs. Force. Hawkins contends that while individuals are substantial or heavy at lower frequencies, they are light and glowing at higher frequencies, when we experience feelings of peace, love, acceptance, and other pleasant emotions that help us comprehend and perceive things more clearly.

According to Hawkins, when you are experiencing lower frequencies, such as 20 (shame), 30 (guilt), 75 (grief), 100 (fear), and 175 (pride), you are more likely to experience illnesses and problems because these emotions are draining and you are more likely to spread emotions like guilt, fear, etc., that drag both you and the people you come into contact with.

You may favorably affect others more when you are operating at higher frequency levels. To back up this idea, the Global

The Princeton University Awareness Project discovered a negative consciousness immediately before the September 21, 2001, attack on the twin towers. On the other hand, it discovered a positive blip prior to President Barack Obama's inauguration, demonstrating that people are impacted by the frequencies of the combined energy of individuals have an impact on the universe as a whole and the earth.

Adapting Mental Patterns

If you want to successfully lessen the influence of your ego in your decision-making and interactions with others, you must shift your thought patterns through increasing brain waves. This does not necessarily mean that your frequency will increase.

So how can you discover your wealth frequency? Naturally, changing your thought habits to ones that enable you to think more clearly and objectively is the first step. The second is that you make an effort to free yourself from the emotional vibrations that are holding you back. Acceptance, peace, love, willingness, and courage are all positive emotions that belong to higher frequencies and allow you to have a more favorable influence on others.

An Individual working at the 300 frequency level can counterbalance 90,000 people operating below the 200 level, whereas an individual operating at the 600 frequency level (peace) can counterbalance 10,000,000 people operating below the 200 level, according to a similar study.

Your key to discovering your wealth frequency is your ability to influence others. It does not imply that you will not encounter failures, but since you are in tune with higher levels of consciousness and have clarity of thought, achieving prosperity is much simpler than when you are functioning in the energy-sucking frequency levels.

Chapter 2:

What is financial abundance?

With the right attitude and behaviors, you can still have the life you've always wanted. Achieve financial abundance if you want to be free from any financial troubles. It is incredible what it is and what it can accomplish for your life. So, these are the things you should know regarding financial plenty.

Being in a scenario where you have just enough money to get by and a little extra for comfort is what is meant by financial abundance.

There is a sense of affluence and freedom from financial worries and burdens, and stress and pressure are not an issue. You can adhere to these crucial elements in order to achieve financial abundance:

What Is Abundance Financial?

1. **Develop Your Mind's Potential**

Develop an abundant mindset by practicing it. Learn from this that material possessions like money shouldn't be used to buy happiness. Of course, everyone requires money, right? Because of how different this bountiful mindset is, it should be used to balance your life. Don't let greed get the better of you. Instead, enjoy your money by setting aside some and contributing to the less fortunate. That makes your motivation so much more positive, and it will eventually coincide with your objectives. This is what is meant by "feeling good."

2. Acquire Knowledge

This is not just for academic levels. In actuality, many wealthy individuals lack the understanding that poor people do. This knowledge entails finding methods to apply what you have learnt (from school or personal experience). This understanding will then be translated into your capacity, and your capacity will be able to provide you with material abundance. Living a life you are enthusiastic about contributes to an abundant existence. With this, you finally have a way to profit from it.

3. Generosity as a Practice

As you pursue your goals in life, assist others in realizing their aspirations. We get back what we give, which is one of many sayings about giving that is true. This does not imply that being generous means giving money. Yes, it is possible, but success does not depend just on financial resources. Create a favorable environment to receive what you want in order to live comfortably and abundantly. Now, this proves the proverb that it is always better to give than to get.

4. The Investment Method

Don't hoard your money too much. In truth, saving money does not guarantee that you will lead a prosperous life. Saving money for emergencies and unforeseen costs is crucial, but you shouldn't use it to lessen your financial load. The thing you should do is invest. Invest in something that will bring you a sizable return in a set amount of time. There is a good probability that doing that will enable you to supplement your current income.

Chapter 3:

The Benefits and Frequency of Wealth

The Vibrational Law

According to the law of vibration, everything in the cosmos is just energy that vibrates at various frequencies. Everything vibrates to a particular pulse, whether it is physical matter or the invisible (such as spirit, chi, etc.).

According to the worldview, the continuum of energies and frequencies contains all that exists. The wealth frequency is one component of that. You may increase the presence of that condition in your life by being able to connect with and resonate at that tone.

Calibration by David Hawkins

David Hawkins proposed calibrating human energy and emotions starting at frequencies between 20 and 1000. States like guilt (30), hatred, grief, love, and peace are in the 500–600 range, and the lower frequencies are dense.

Starting at 200 (courage), the first positive emotion is calibrated, and goes up from there. You must resonate these individual bits starting at 200 and upwards in order to achieve the circumstances and minute elements making up the concept of "wealth."

The calibration is unimportant; rather, we can use that figure as a reference to calibrate the range of human emotions or states up or down to get the desired results.

Law of Attraction and Resonance

Though they have some similarities, the laws of attraction and resonance are different. Generic resonance with wealth will draw the circumstances that lead to financial prosperity because there are several types of wealth thoughts and ideas.

The difference between whether you will attract more of one thing over another depends on the rule of resonance. The law of resonance, for instance, distinguishes between whether you can manifest a chair or a table even though both belong to the general category of "furniture."

Broadcasting of Wealth on Purposeful Frequencies

You can increase the likelihood of attracting favorable circumstances for wealth by training your mind to live in this frequency and charge it with intensity and resonance, teaching the same to everyone in your environment, such as employees and business partners, and even charging the physical space you are in.

Due to the fact that this is not how we typically think, feel, or perceive the world, it may first need a lot of conscious effort to enter that state of mind. It will start to feel more natural with time, and eventually it will become your default frequency or condition.

What Midas did

The "Midas touch" phenomena begins to appear in your life once you have developed a natural resonance with this frequency. Everything that you touch just seems to function effortlessly and naturally without any conscious effort on your part!

One theory for why success spawns success is that way. One accomplishment opens the way for subsequent triumphs, and so on, creating a success momentum.

Metaphor for the Immune System

Anybody who has achieved the highest levels of success has cultivated a natural ability to think and act in these frequencies. When things don't go as planned, they are unnatural and flushed out, like when the immune system gets rid of the invaders.

Diseases are negativities, while positive frequencies (for riches) are the immune system's automatic antibody super soldiers.

Chapter 4

Bringing Together Complementary Patterns

If you dig deep enough, you will discover that everything in the cosmos is just energy and that all energy is just vibrations, and that it is these vibrating patterns that give gases their properties as gases, liquids their properties as liquids, and solids their properties as solids. Included in this are immaterial like spirit and soul. Viewing the different states of matter in order, starting with ether, then moving through spirit/soul, gases, liquids, and solids, may be useful.

Although some people claim to be able to move heavy objects with their minds alone through telekinesis, this does not mean you can actually move heavy objects with just your mind. This book is not intended to cover that.

Making a channel of least resistance where a manifestation is achievable and is a better pathway than the opposite of what we desire is the goal of manifestation through attracting suitable energy patterns.

A Justification for Good and Bad Luck

"Luck is when opportunity meets preparation" - Seneca

If you generate within yourself and without the conditions that make an occurrence more likely to occur, something we would refer to as "luck," the said luck would have to be simpler to materialize over a setting full of negativity and forces that suggest otherwise, conditions making up "poor luck."

Many people believe that "The Secret" is merely wishful thinking and not taking action because of how popular it has become in recent months. Energy is also used in action. It is a part of force, a physical force that employs the ethereal energy and vibrational configurations made to bring about events in the physical world.

Real-World Applications of Energy Utilization

There is just the drawing of perfect circumstances, characters, and occurrences. Compared to the more powerful physical activities, the results produced through this channel are more potent in the subtler, ethereal realms. It is not practical to physically move a ton-weighted object using these methods. You require mechanical power, equipment, and gadgets like a crane in order to do this.

How can one materialize a crane, too?

You only need to contact the business that rents out large industrial machinery. Within the heavy machinery industry, you can socialize and establish acquaintances. You can pretend to already have the crane by doing a careful visualization. To achieve that goal, layer as many working techniques as you can, rather than just employing one on top of another.

I seriously doubt that you could summon a crane by yourself, much less cause a heavy object to levitate to a different position. Simply said, it is built on fantasy and is not reality.

Establishing Complementary Patterns for Wealth and Abundance

The above illustration refers to a highly particular goal that may be achieved by mechanical devices, such as a crane. However, we cannot just limit an issue to just one element like the crane since designing a general living situation with numerous different factors, avenues of approach, and results is not conceivable. And this is where it might be helpful to employ the law of attraction, which states that like attracts like.

We may attract coincidences, people, and resources that otherwise wouldn't appear to us by accident if we cultivate the correct vibrations and energies inside ourselves and our enterprises. We are able to attract and maintain these variables in our area because we have developed the proper energy signatures.

In conclusion, it involves developing the proper energies to attract resources and building a sustainable framework so that resources and assets may be preserved naturally in our area of influence where they are helpful. There is nothing to lose by tapping into this reservoir of power that is available to all of us, even if it exists in the realm of intangibles and cannot be measured with our earthly scientific apparatus.

Chapter 5

Understanding Your Vibrational Hum.

Everything emits small vibrations that only those who look for them can detect. Living a wealthy and full life requires an awareness of vibrations, including your own. Positive and negative vibrations or energy are the two different forms. As you are undoubtedly aware, good energy empowers you to influence others and accomplish more, but bad energy drags you down along with those around you.

Identification of Vibrations

Once you've mastered the ability to recognize vibrations, or energy as some people prefer to refer to it, be sure to only connect with good vibes since doing so will assist your own vibrations rise. Stay away from unfavorable vibes that might weaken or reduce your own.

Learn how to identify and categorize vibrations as the first step in taking use of the power that is continually discharged into the environment. This may be accomplished using a tested technique. Consider the trembling that you experience while a train is moving down its tracks. You may still feel the vibrations of a train even when one may not really be running.

You can perceive your surroundings if you are at ease and have your senses open to them. You'll ultimately have the patience necessary to notice them, but it will take some time. It might assist to practice meditation techniques that include blocking out the background noise of daily living. Keep your eyes open and eventually you will be able to see them. When you're meditating, you're not concentrating. To take use of vibrations' abilities, you must develop the sense of hearing.

Being Aware of Your Own Vibrations

The next thing to do is to focus on yourself once you have mastered the capacity to sense and perceive vibrations. It will take some time to do a thorough examination and reflection on your current situation.

Is vibration. Your attitudes toward specific issues that are generally significant to people and to you will reveal what they are. All you have to do is be sincere with yourself.

Knowing your vibrational hum is crucial because it directly affects how you live your life. If you don't know where you are right now, it will be quite difficult for you to achieve your life objectives.

Increasing vibrations

The next thing you do is try to raise your vibrations after assessing where you are in terms of your vibrational hum. There are many methods to do this, and the more you apply yourself, the simpler it will be for you to flourish and lead a full life. Keeping healthy is one of the recognized methods for boosting vibrations. You can boost your vibrations by eating more nutritious foods, staying hydrated, and avoiding foods that are high in toxins. Your vibration will be greatly increased by practicing meditation, learning to unwind, adopting the correct attitudes, and being more focused on your life's passions. In general, your vibes are more upbeat the happier you are.

Your vibrations can be Increased even further by associating your self Only with people with positive vibration.

Chapter 6

What Is Vibrational Equilibrium?

Since you are a vibrational entity, you transmit signals that identify you to other people. Of course, not everyone receives your signals, only those whose signals are in line with yours. There will be two-way communication if you put out pleasant signals and other people who are also happy respond to them. In a vibrational world, that is how vibrational beings communicate. It's known as attracting similar patterns. This fosters peace.

Bringing Together Compatible Patterns

If you understand that you are a vibrating entity, you will want to draw in the positive messages. You need to understand your vibrational hum before you can achieve that. How? You look inside of yourself. You can achieve this by simply relaxing your thoughts, filtering out distracting sounds, and paying attention to the messages your body is emitting.

Do you feel content, unhappy, angry, annoyed, depressed, or happy? Whatever feelings you experience will be reflected in your vibrations or signals, and you also pick up on vibrations from your surroundings.

Equilibrium Vibrational

Your universe is governed by the signals you send out and receive because you are a vibrational creature. You will eventually reach a state of vibrational equilibrium, which is indicated by the dominating signal you transmit and receive.

Although the compatibility offers stability, is it the stability you're looking for? For instance, if you've been struggling financially for years and it's stopped demoralizing or frustrating you, it might only indicate that your vibrational equilibrium is tuned for this kind of existence.

Change in vibration is the only method to disrupt a vibrational balance that keeps you from achieving more, such as greater prosperity.

Your vibrational equilibrium can be changed.

It is difficult to modify vibrations permanently. You can't do it, for example, by getting dressed, having a shower, or working out. The positive emotions you experience as a result of doing these things can momentarily change your frequency.

Your efforts should be concentrated on altering the dominating signals that you release if you want to shift your vibrational equilibrium. Your top priority must be to permanently break contact with the environment that fosters your negative equilibrium; otherwise, you will repeatedly revert to that state.

There are two ways to change your present unfavorable equilibrium to one that is more favorable. The first is to modify your signals so that you can counteract the signals coming from your surroundings.

You can direct your thoughts and energy toward your objectives, and this new focus, which is incompatible with your current surroundings, will gradually alter those surroundings since you will be drawing in new signals. You'll learn new things, see new things, and do new things.

Your new vibrations will eventually match up with your physical reality.

By graphically visualizing your objectives for at least 20 minutes each day, you may effectively avoid your environment from interfering with your attempts to change vibrations. If you put powerful emotions into it, you'll eventually find that the signals you gather up support your vibrations.

Another strategy is to physically or socially withdraw from your current setting. You can achieve this by relocating to an area with different signals or by ceasing to hang out with your carefree and slacker pals.

Your vibrational equilibrium will shift once your vibrations have been altered.

Chapter 7

Changing Your Vibration

Your mind is so strong that it literally has the capacity to manipulate the cosmos. Our words, thoughts, and feelings truly produce an undetectable vibration that transmits energy.

The quantum space, where everything is possible and anybody can succeed, is where this energy is currently conspiring. You are therefore seen as an energetic entity as well, not just due to physical characteristics but also due to your capacity for both receiving and transmitting energy. Willingness to succeed in life then discover how to change your vibration.

What you want is not what matters.

Thoughts, feelings, and dreams may bring vibrations to your life, but that does not guarantee that you will receive them. The most important factor is how you are telling the universe to send you what you desire; these are only a few components of it. As you continue to trade energy, you will eventually experience signal interruption due to unpredictable events because you are always creating vibes. In order to accomplish that, you must align every aspect of your life with your goals and ward off everyone who would stand in your way.

Therefore, it sends out a bad message if a particular circumstance makes you feel dissatisfied, angry, or demotivated. Avoid it by surrounding yourself with upbeat individuals and putting forth positive energy that will make you feel good in any situation.

Need to Be Aware of Your Vibration

As you practice a technique to build inner peace, become more in touch with who you are. Keep your thoughts at a low volume and pay attention to your body to renew positive vibrations. Whatever you choose to name it—prayer, meditation, whatever—is acceptable. Simply said, you need to stop thinking and concentrate on being calm and tranquil.

You can take a leisurely stroll along the beach or simply go on vacation outside of the city. You can even have a relaxing, private "me" time in your own room for practical reasons. Let your emotions flow as you quiet yourself.

Come in. Feel everything, let it all out by crying if you can, and get it all out of your system. Recognize your body's messages. There may be times when you experience a range of emotions, including extreme sadness followed by feelings of solace and tranquility. You occasionally feel incredibly joyful and alive. Feel their presence and their resonance.

The Change in Vibration

You may now adjust your vibration in the direction of you r objective since you are more equipped to understand how vibrations affect your mind and how to detect them. The first thing you can do is turn off any environments that interfere with your signal. Never allow yourself to think negatively or even to be around negatively. Here's a helpful hint: spend 15 minutes each day visualizing your objective.

Feel your emotions deeply, and soon you'll be able to tune into your vibrations and learn how to ward off obstacles in your path. The next action you may take is to proactively alter your environment. You can go hang out with others who share your ambitious aspirations, alter the design of your home, or even alter your appearance. All these should make you feel good and create a strong vibration.

Chapter 8

Creating What You Want

By this point in the book, you should be aware that altering your perspective and entire way of thinking is necessary if you desire a more fulfilling existence. Additional advice on how to produce and obtain what you desire is provided below:

Tips

Tip #1: Keep Your Attention on What Is Important

Think positively instead of negatively because if you do, you will never have enough. This is a really simple tip that, if followed, will have a big beneficial impact on your life. Your life will change drastically if you alter your concentration and what you are focused on.

Your mind and soul will continue to believe that you are without something if you concentrate on what you do not have. On the other hand, when you practice being thankful for what you DO have on a regular basis, you can teach the good energies around you to give you what you want.

You will be able to find solutions to both ordinary and uncommon situations in your life with this kind of mentality. You'll be more receptive to the good vibes and chances that are all around you, which will make winning simpler.

Tip #2: Adopt a new definition of failure

Fear of failing is one of the things that prevents people from accomplishing great things. We all experience this at some point in our life. We are terrified to fail and we are afraid to endure the consequences of failing.

However, things will significantly alter for you, including your perspective on failing, once you redefine failure in a more positive way.

Do not accept failure as a possibility. Instead, consider failure as a chance to learn and improve on what you just done. Without failure, we would not be the people and things that we are today. So view failure as a stepping stone to achieving your goals rather than something bigger than you that scares you. Teach your mind to reframe failure as an opportunity to grow as a person rather than as a depressing, negative occurrence.

Tip #3: You are in control of yourself.

Who exactly is your employer? Your employer should be YOU alone. Whatever you want to happen in your life is entirely up to you. You alone are accountable for your actions. You will grow older and be motivated to make better decisions for yourself if you acknowledge and embrace the truth that no one else can assist you in creating your successful future.

Chapter 9

Learn the distinction between desire and detachment

Despite having the best intentions and skills, many people nevertheless end up not getting what they want due to misunderstandings regarding these two concepts: desire and detachment.

The first thing you need to understand about the two is that they are not completely at odds with one another. They are linked together, though, since they have the power to either make the Law of Attraction operate in your favor or not.

The majority of individuals equate this state with needing or desiring something. However, where the Law of Attractions is concerned, desire is more than that. In fact, the most effective approach to understand the significance of desire in a person's life is to see it as the outcome of having personal preferences.

Just what is desire?

Finding out what you don't want in your life can help you identify what you do. Because of this, realizing that you dislike sour food may later cause you to realize that you enjoy sweet or spicy food instead. You could think of these inclinations as desires. To put it another way, you just prefer spicy cuisine to foods with a sour flavor.

Another common misconception is that desire is immoral. Because they can result in avarice, selfishness, jealously, and many other undesirable feelings, some people view desires as being "bad." But once again, they are mistaken there.

Think about the prior instance. Is it wicked, sinful, or immoral to prefer spicy food to sour food?

Additionally, there are numerous wants that are difficult to categorize as wicked or, even worse, wrong. Some folks only want to be in good health. Some people might want to be in a position to assist those in need.

Detachment

However, whether coupled by emotions of attachment…or detachment, desire can boomerang and lead to your demise.

• Attachment – Your desire is so intense that it causes you to experience unpleasant feelings as a result. Regarding your ability to reach your objective, you experience pressure. You are concerned and afraid of what will happen if you don't get what you want.

• Detachment – You are simply concerned with your desires. There is nothing else you experience. You are unable to feel sympathy or empathy for the suffering of others feelings because everything in you is completely focused in obtaining what you desire.

Take a kid who wants to get good grades as an example. The student may become so preoccupied with worrying about test outcomes due to attachment feelings that he develops panic attacks and insomnia. However, a student who shares the same goal might turn to detachment as a coping strategy. In this instance, the student spends all of his time studying to the exclusion of everything else, including regular eating and sleeping schedules and the treatment of family members.

Obviously, desire and detachment are two different emotions, yet you can feel both at once. In the end, if you want your wishes to be satisfied, you should strive towards nonattachment. You are liberated from unfavorable ideas and feelings by nonattachment feelings, while simultaneously inspiring you to act and think more wisely in order to accomplish your goal.

Summary

How to Plan for Financial Abundance: Benefits

Some of you might be of the opinion that you are fully knowledgeable about how to maintain the best mindset and attitude for experiencing financial abundance at this point. That's all well and good, but you must remember that obtaining financial abundance also necessitates taking wise, calculated, realistic, and concrete steps. It is at this point that planning begins.

A Financial Abundance Plan: 6 Steps to Follow

In order to create, finish, and perfect planning, a process must be followed. Choose the best strategy by taking your time. If you make changes after plans are finalized, it will be harder and more expensive to put them into effect.

Step 1: Increasing Cash Flow

Increasing your cash flow should be the first objective of your strategy. It might not imply greater revenue, profit, or sales, but it does imply greater financial adaptability. Cutting costs directly is another way to improve your cash flow. You also give yourself better leverage for resolving issues if you have more money on hand.

Using opportunities to make money and unforeseen financial crises

.

Step 2: Investment in Healthcare and Insurance

Health issues are one of the biggest sources of costs, so be sure to invest in healthcare plans and insurance now to avoid headaches in the future.

Speaking of insurance, it is also recommended to insure the majority of your possessions, if not all of them, is worth protecting because it has value. Consider purchasing life insurance that pays out reasonably well as well.

Step 3: Managing and eliminating debt

Stop putting off the inevitable; the time has come. Nowadays, debts are rarely forgiven. Most of the time, there is no way to avoid them, so it is best to get serious and decide which debts are most important and which ones merit further discussion with the relevant creditors. This is not to say that debt is always a bad thing, of course. Debt can increase cash flow and allow you to take advantage of uncommon investment opportunities. Just make sure you only borrow what you actually need or, at the very least, what you can afford to pay back.

Step 4: higher savings

There is no need to explain this further, I think. The best way to secure your retirement and overall future is probably to start saving. Just remember that saving can take many different forms, so make an informed decision!

Step 5: Make investments

In any strategy for achieving financial abundance, passive income is a necessity. Investments are unquestionably one of the most lucrative, but they can also be one of the riskiest, forms of passive income. When selecting an investment to trust with your hard-earned money, exercise caution.

Step 6: Planning your estate

Last but not least, it is never too late to begin making plans for what will happen to your estate if, for any reason, you are unable to manage it. You can write your own will and ensure that it is valid and airtight on your own, of course, but only if you are prepared to invest the time necessary to learn all there is to know about estate planning.

The aforementioned actions are undoubtedly easier said than done, but if you stick to your own plan, they will open the door to financial abundance.

www.ingramcontent.com/pod-product-compliance
Lightning Source LLC
Chambersburg PA
CBHW050307220526
45465CB00002B/865